WITCH HUNTER

3-4

JUNG-MAN CHO

WITCH HUNTER

VOLUME 3-4

story &
art by Jung-man Cho

STAFF CREDITS

translation	ChanHee Grace Sung
adaptation	Rebecca Scoble
lettering	Wacky Eloriaga-Dunglao
layout	Bambi Eloriaga-Amago
cover design	Nicky Lim
editor	Adam Arnold
publisher	Jason DeAngelis
	Seven Seas Entertainment

WITCH HUNTER VOL. 3-4
©2006, 2007 by CHO Jung-man, Daewon C.I. Inc. All rights reserved.
First published in Korea in 2006, 2007 by Daewon C.I. Inc. English translation
rights arranged by Daewon C.I. Inc. through Topaz Agency Inc.

ISBN: 978-1-935934-98-1

Printed in the USA

First Printing: October 2012

10 9 8 7 6 5 4 3 2 1

Seven Seas

FOLLOW US ONLINE: **www.gomanga.com**

PREVIOUSLY...

Witches and humans lived together in peace, until the witches declared war. In the blink of an eye, the witches conquered two-thirds of the world, leaving unparalleled destruction in their wake. To survive, the remaining free countries gathered exceptional humans with special powers in an international agency—the Witch Hunters.

Tasha Godspell, aka "The Marksman," is an A-Class Witch Hunter. He and his pumpkin-headed supporter Halloween fight witches to protect humans. But he carries a dark secret—the witch who destroyed his hometown was none other than his sister, Aria. Tasha fought the shadow-controlling witch Varete for a chance to take his sister back, but Varete and Aria escaped.

Later, Tasha and his comrades Xing and Tarras came across a village under the thrall of a mind-controlling witch. Xing and Tarras quickly fell under the witch's control, but everyone was in for a surprise when Monica, who'd seemed like an ordinary girl, awakened as a witch right in front of them!

HEY... UM, TASHA?

I WANTED TO ASK YOU SOMETHING...

WHAT IS IT?

YOU SAID WE'RE GOING TO A **STATION**, RIGHT?

YEAH.

SO, HOW COME...

TWITCH

TWITCH

...WE'RE IN THE MIDDLE OF A FREAKIN' DESERT?!

FWSSH TAH FWSSH TAH TAH

BECAUSE THERE'S A STATION OUT HERE, OBVIOUSLY.

OBVIOUSLY!

If you're gonna lie, at least put some effort into it!

NOBODY'D PUT A STATION ALL THE WAY OUT *HERE*! IT DOESN'T MAKE ANY SENSE!

Are you stupid?!

THERE IT IS.

POINT

WHAT?!

......

WHAT'S THAT SUPPOSED TO BE?

W·H EXPRESS

CAN'T YOU SEE IT? IT'S THE STATION SIGN.

THIS IS WHAT YOU DRAGGED ME OUT HERE FOR?

OF COURSE.

THERE'S NOTHING HERE! HOW THE HECK IS *THIS* A STATION?!

Now I'm stranded in the desert with a moron!

JUST LOOK THROUGH YOUR SUPPORTER... UNLESS THAT THING'S JUST A GAUDY ACCESSORY.

YEAH, RIGHT. LIKE THAT'S GOING TO MAKE A--

OH.

Aah!

9. STATION

LET ME PRESENT...

...THE EXCLUSIVE WH TRANSPORTER, "THE IRON STALLION." HEAVILY CONCEALED BY MAGIC, IT CAN ONLY BE SEEN BY AN ELITE FEW!

Plus, it's free!

WHAT'RE YOU PUNKS DOING HERE?!

APPARENTLY, CENTRAL REGISTERED THE THREE OF US AS A TEAM.

HEY, TASHA. HOPE YOU DON'T MIND WE ALREADY MADE OURSELVES AT HOME.

YOU'VE GOT TO BE KIDDING ME!

THIS CAN'T BE HAPPENING! I-I'LL MAKE THEM FIX IT! THEY CAN'T JUST...

ME, TEAMED UP WITH A HUGE PERVERT AND KING NARCISSIST...

TREMBLE

TREMBLE

King Narcissist?

Pervert?

DON'T THINK YOU'RE THE ONLY ONE DEMANDING A CHANGE.

HOW COULD THEY PUT A GIFTED WH LIKE MYSELF IN A GROUP WITH YOU TWO?

WE NEED TO DISSOLVE THIS PARTNERSHIP BEFORE MY REPUTATION IS TARNISHED.

GIFTED WH? REALLY?

THERE'S NOTHING EITHER OF YOU CAN DO RIGHT NOW. WHY DON'T YOU JUST **RELAX**?

YOU CAN SIT OVER HERE.

POFF

REALLY? I THOUGHT A PLAYBOY LIKE YOU WOULD WANT MONICA TO SIT WITH YOU FOR SURE.

ME?

WHAT DO YOU TAKE ME FOR?

SHE ISN'T A WOMAN! WHERE ARE THE BOOBS? *BOOBS?!*

POINT

UH, SURE, I'LL SIT THERE.

YOU CRAPPY JERK!

POW

TINY BOOBS!

YOU SEEM UNUSUALLY CHEERFUL.

YEAH, WELL, SOMETIMES YOUR IDIOCY IS FUN.

UM... WELL...

I WANTED TO THANK YOU.

HUH? WHAT FOR?

FOR WHAT YOU SAID EARLIER...

I SAID...?

OH!

ZP

I ONLY SAID IT BECAUSE IT'S TRUE.

SO DON'T WORRY ABOUT IT.

NO! HOW DID YOU...?

MY SUPPORTER IS INVISIBLE! HOW COULD HE HIT IT LIKE THAT?

FSSSSSH

THIS STRANGE FIELD HAS ENORMOUS MAGICAL ENERGY...

HOW CAN A MERE HUMAN POSSESS SO MUCH POWER?

WHEN I'M INSIDE THE FIELD, MY GUN CAN DETECT THE ENEMY'S SOUND, TEMPERATURE, MANA--EVEN EVIL INTENTIONS.

THE ONLY DRAWBACK IS THAT IT TAKES A HUGE AMOUNT OF MANA TO CONJURE AND MAINTAIN.

THAT WAS MY MAGIC BATTLE-FIELD.

THAT'S THE DUMBEST THING I'VE EVER **HEARD**! YOU PATHETIC HUMANS CAN'T USE MAGIC!

YOU DON'T EVEN HAVE A **WITCH'S HAT**!

YOU'RE RIGHT. HUMANS CAN'T USE MAGIC.

HUH?

THAT'S WHERE THIS COMES IN-- MY DIMENSIONAL GALLERY POUCH.

TA-DA

IT'S A MAGIC ITEM MADE BY MY TEACHER, EDEA FLORENCE. BETTER KNOWN AS "THE WHITE WITCH."

IT'S GOT ENOUGH SPECIAL ABILITIES TO MAKE A MEDIOCRE KID LIKE ME INTO A **STAR WH.**

I'M SORRY, YOU SAID YOU WERE CONTROLLING A HUMAN? OH, BY THE WAY, **MONICA'S** PROTECTING THE REST OF US, SO GOOD LUCK **FINDING** ANOTHER PUPPET.

HSSSSSSSS

SORRY, TARRAS.

SACRIFICING YOU WAS THE ONLY WAY WE COULD WIN.

JUST BE GRATEFUL I USED A **TRANQUILIZER,** BECAUSE I WAS SOOO TEMPTED TO USE LIVE ROUNDS.

THE WORLD'S MOST TERRIBLE PRISON FOR WITCHES. NO ONE HAS EVER ESCAPED!

THE ISLAND THAT DRAINS ALL MAGIC.

NO. I'LL DIE FIRST.

HEY!

HEY, YOU!

YEAH! HELP ME OUT!

ME?

QUICK, RELEASE YOUR DISPEL!

THINK ABOUT IT. YOU KNOW THE PEOPLE AROUND HERE. YOU *KNOW* HOW RELIGIOUS THEY ARE.

DEATH TO ALL WITCHES.

AND WHAT'S THEIR MOST FUNDAMENTAL BELIEF?

BA-BMP

DO YOU THINK THEY'LL ACCEPT YOU WHEN THEY SEE WHAT YOU ARE?

IF YOU'RE LUCKY, THEY'LL EXILE YOU. BUT LET'S BE REALISTIC...

IT'S *MUCH* MORE LIKELY THAT YOU'LL BE BURNED ALIVE.

AND THAT'S NOT ALL.

YOU MUST'VE NOTICED THE "CIRCLE-CROSS" ON YOUR COMPANION'S CLOTHES--THAT SAME RELIGIOUS SYMBOL.

THEY'RE CALLED **WITCH HUNTERS** FOR A REASON, YOU KNOW.

DO YOU REALLY THINK THEY'LL JUST LET YOU GO?

THERE'S A **TRADITION** AMONG WITCHES. A BABY WITCH LIKE YOURSELF WILL TEAM UP WITH A VETERAN LIKE ME, WHO'LL GUIDE AND **TEACH** YOU. SURVIVAL IS MUCH EASIER AS A TEAM.

ONCE THEY'RE DONE USING YOU, YOU'LL BE HUNTED DOWN, TOO.

SO, WHAT DO YOU THINK? WOULDN'T IT BE BETTER TO SIDE WITH SOMEONE WHO CAN HELP YOU GROW AND **THRIVE** AS A WITCH, INSTEAD OF THE ENEMIES OF OUR KIND?

...IN ALCATRAZ.

YES.

RIGHT. PLEASE CONNECT ME TO CENTRAL.

THE MAGIC LINE HAS BEEN DISCONNECTED. BEEP~!

SO, TRANSFERRING THE WITCH WENT SMOOTHLY?

YEAH. ALCATRAZ RECEIVED HER WITHOUT ANY PROBLEMS.

HEY, UM, XING?

I THINK IT'S TIME TO GO.

NOW THAT THE SCREAMING'S STARTED...

LOOKS LIKE THE PEOPLE WHO RAN FROM THE FIGHT ARE ALL COMING BACK NOW.

My house! Waah!

Nooo! My store!

My farm! My beautiful farm!

OH BOY. WELL, WE *DID* WRECK THEIR TOWN, SO I GET WHY THEY'RE UPSET...

WE? HEY, DON'T LUMP ME IN THERE WITH YOU. I BARELY DESTROYED ANYTHING!

WELL, WE'RE STILL IN UNIFORM, SO WE SHOULD BE ABLE TO SLIP AWAY AS LONG AS WE KEEP A LOW PROFI--

YOU SLIMY WH PUNKS!

HUH?

I PAID YOU SO THIS *WOULDN'T* HAPPEN! LOOK AT MY STORE!!

THAT LITTLE WEASEL SCAMMED ME! I CLEANED OUT MY COFFERS FOR HIM!

DON'T YOU *DARE* TRY TO SNEAK AWAY!

I GUESS YOU WERE BUSY THIS AFTERNOON...

KU-KLAK

XIIING? YOU WOULDN'T RAT ME OUT TO CENTRAL, RIGHT? *RIGHT?!*

SMUSH

IS THAT HOW YOU ASK FOR A FAVOR?

MORE IMPORTANTLY, WHAT ARE WE GOING TO DO ABOUT *THAT?*

HM?

IT'S A WITCH!

WITCH!

W

OH CRA

SHE MUST BE THE ONE THE WHs CAPTURED.

HANG ON, ISN'T THAT... MONICA?

MONICA?! SHE'S THE ONE WHO DESTROYED OUR VILLAGE?!

SHE MURDERE OUR PEOPLE!

SO, THAT MEANS SHE'S POWERLESS NOW?

SHE'S EVIL!

DO YOU THINK THEY'LL ACCEPT YOU WHEN THEY SEE WHAT YOU ARE?

NO! THEY'LL
UNDERSTAND
ONCE I
EXPLAIN!

OW!

I
D-DIDN'T
DO THIS!

MASTER,
YOU'RE IN
DANGER. PLEASE
TRANSFER SOME
MANA TO ME.

I CAN'T!
THEY'LL
NEVER
BELIEVE
ME IF
I DO!

IT
WASN'T ME!
I SWEAR!

PLEASE!
PLEASE, JUST
LISTEN--!

SHE'S A
WITCH!

WITCH!

I DIDN'T DO
ANYTHING!

WHY WON'T
YOU LET ME
EXPLAIN?!

SCREE~

TP

AHH~! IT'S BEEN A WHIL SINCE I'VE BEEN BACK THE WESTER DISTRICT CENTER.

TASHA GODSPELL.

Cool, right?

Whoa...

YEAH?

WE'VE COME FROM CENTRA TO FIND YOU.

DOOM

THEY'RE FROM CENTRAL? BUT ONLY *JUDICIAL MEMBERS* ACTUALLY WORK THERE...

SO...WHAT DOES THE JUDICIAL OFFICE NEED FROM ME?

TASHA GODSPELL, YOU ARE UNDER ARREST FOR THE **MURDER** OF A WH.

WHAT ...?

IF THEY DIDN'T BECOME WHS...

LOAN SHARK.

PAY UP NOW, BEFORE THINGS GET... UNPLEAS-ANT.

FLASH SPEED DELIVERY!

SELLS HIS OWN LINE OF SCANNERS!

NOTHING BEATS EARTH SCAN!

AND HALLOWEEN...

LINDA!

LINDA!

ALISHA?

BIG NEWS! ONE OF YOUR WHs, MR. GODSPELL, HAS RETURNED!

TASHA? REALLY? HE HASN'T BEEN BACK HERE IN QUITE A WHILE.

TMP

TMP

TMP

HEE HEE! BUT THERE'S MORE TO IT THAN THAT!

HM?

10. EVIDENCE/PROOF

HOWEVER, SINCE THERE ARE FOUR A-CLASS WHs PRESENT...

TDUN

DUUUN

ALL JUDGMENTS AND SENTENCES HANDED DOWN IN THIS SUMMARY TRIAL WILL BE CONSIDERED BINDING.

TWO WEEKS AGO, THE **FORTE WITCH**, ALSO KNOWN AS **SHOUT**, WAS DISCOVERED DEAD.

THE MAIN SUSPECT IS TASHA GODSPELL.

ANY OBJEC- TIONS...

TASHA GODSPELL?

HMPH. THIS IS ABSURD.

WHEN WHs DIE, IT'S ALWAYS A WITCH. WHY ARE YOU TRYING TO BLAME THIS ON ME?

THIS IS THE SCENE OF SHOUT'S MURDER.

BAM

I'M SURE YOU UNDERSTAND WHAT THIS PHOTO *PROVES.*

TASHA... SEE THE BULLET HOLES ALONG THE BROKEN WALLS?

TP

THOSE HOLES COULD ONLY BE MADE BY HIGH LEVEL MAGIC.

AND THERE'S ONLY ONE WEAPON THAT CAN PRODUCE THAT KIND OF BULLETS...

FLICK

FLIP

THIS MANA GUN.

FOR A WHILE, I RESEARCHED THIS GUN IN THE HOPES OF MASS PRODUCING THEM.

THE GUN ITSELF-- ITS SHAPE AND DESIGN-- WAS EASY TO REPLICATE...

BUT I COULD NEVER GET THE GUNS TO PRODUCE BULLETS FROM MANA, AT LEAST NOT FAST ENOUGH TO BE USEFUL.

I TRIED AND **FAILED** MANY TIMES BEFORE GIVING UP.

THIS GUN MAY LOOK SIMPLE, BUT IT TOOK A HUGE AMOUNT OF MAGIC AND SKILL TO CREATE. IN FACT, THERE'S ONLY ONE WITCH I KNOW OF WHO'S EVER MANAGED TO MAKE ONE.

JUST ONE PERSON...

THE MASTER OF MAGIC SCIENCE, **EDEA FLORENCE.** SHE'S THE ONLY PERSON WHO COULD'VE MADE THIS GUN.

ALL THE EVIDENCE POINTS TO YOU.

SINCE SHE'S DEAD, WE KNOW THERE'S ONLY ONE MANA GUN IN EXISTENCE. THE ONE THAT BELONGS TO **YOU, TASHA.**

HEE HEE... MASTER OF MAGICAL SCIENCE, YEAH RIGHT.

ECLIPSE, I HAVE A QUESTION.

SURE, WHAT'S UP?

BZZZZT

DID THAT GUY JUST INSULT YOU?

HM... I GUESS HE DID.

OKAY, THEN CAN I...

UM...

IT'S GONNA BE OKAY, RIGHT?

OF COURSE. ANYBODY CAN SEE THAT TASHA WOULDN'T *MURDER* SOMEONE.

EXCEPT MAYBE FOR MONEY...

I WONDER WHAT'S GOING ON INSIDE!

THEY WON'T LET TEAM MEMBERS IN! IT'S DRIVING ME CRAZY!

I OVERHEARD SOME GUYS WALKING BY...

THEY SAID IT ISN'T LOOKING GOOD FOR TASHA.

WHAT SHOULD WE DO?

TMP

TMP

I NEVER THOUGHT I'D LIVE TO SEE THE DAY! XING AND TARRAS, SITTING PEACEFULLY TOGETHER?

YOU...

UGH, NOBODY WANTS TO SEE THIS GUY AGAIN.

THE COURT RECOGNIZES AMOS OF BLACK STAR. EXPLAIN YOURSELF.

CLOK CLOK

EXACTLY TWO WEEKS AGO...

TASHA WAS WITH MY TEAM, WITCH HUNTING IN SINTRA.

POINT

...?

THERE WAS A WITCH HIDING AT SINTRA AND WE HAD SOME TROUBLE TAKING HER DOWN. LUCKILY, TASHA WAS IN THE AREA, SO WE INITIATED HELP.

WE KNEW TASHA'S BATTLEFIELD COULD DETECT THE HIDDEN WITCH.

IF YOU DON'T BELIEVE ME, SEND SOMEONE TO SINTRA. THERE SHOULD STILL BE REMNANTS OF TASHA'S BULLETS TO BE FOUND.

WE DIDN'T REPORT THIS EARLIER BECAUSE WE **FAILED** TO CAPTURE THE WITCH. HOWEVER, SINTRA AND THE PLACE YOU FOUND SHOUT'S BODY ARE NOWHERE NEAR EACH OTHER.

TO BE IN **BOTH** PLACES ON THE SAME DAY, HE'D NEED TO USE MAGIC PORTALS.

AND IF HE DID THAT, YOU'D HAVE THE PORTAL **DOCUMENTS** SAYING SO, CORRECT?

HM, I'M SURE NO ONE REQUESTED THAT LONG A DISTANCE THAT DAY...

OF COURSE NOT. PLUS, WE ALL KNOW TASHA **CAN'T** TELEPORT WITHOUT USING A MAGIC PORTAL.

SO, HE'S IN THE CLEAR NOW, RIGHT?

I DON'T THINK SO.

HOW DO WE KNOW THAT YOU AND TASHA AREN'T **PARTNERS** IN THIS?

YOU COULD JUST BE **COVERING** FOR HIM.

WHAT
?!!

THIS TRIAL IS
POSTPONED UNTIL
FURTHER NOTICE.

TASHA GODSPELL
WILL REMAIN
HERE UNDER
SURVEILLANCE UNTIL
THE COURT CAN
RECONVENE.

THE
SITUATION
IS VERY
DIRE.

HE WILL NOT
PARTICIPATE IN
MISSIONS FOR
THE TIME
BEING.

UGH.

HOW...

HOW DID A MASTER CON ARTIST LIKE ME GET BLACKMAILED BY A GUY LIKE *THAT?*

TURN

TASHA!!

MONICA!

Oh, and the hangers-on...

THANK GOODNESS...

Who're you calling hangers-on?!

I WAS REALLY WORRIED!

SORRY ABOUT THAT.

HEY, TASHA!

ECLIPSE! ALV!

HI!

TASHA, I'M SO RELIEVED YOU DIDN'T DO IT! LAST THINK I EVER WANT TO DO IS THROW LADY FLORENCE'S STUDENT INTO PRISON.

OOH! IS SHE THE NEW WITCH YOU BROUGHT BACK?

YUP.

HMM...

WOW, VERY IMPRESSIVE. THIS GIRL POSSESSES A SUPPORTER OF COMMONERS.

SHE'S ONLY THE SECOND PERSON I'VE EVER SEEN WITH ONE--AND THE FIRST WAS RAN, YOUR OTHER DISCOVERY.

IT'S AMAZIN' TASHA--YOU' ONLY EVER BROUGHT TW WITCHES BA TO THE CENTER, YE THEY BOT HAVE A SUPER-RAF SPIRITUAL SUPPORTEF

ALV.

CREAK

FFMP

HAH.

WHAT IS GOING ON...?

ECLIPSE HAD IT RIGHT...

MY TEACHER, MS. EDEA, WAS THE ONLY PERSON WHO COULD CREATE A MANA GUN.

BUT THOSE BULLET HOLES...IT'S THE ONLY THING THAT COULD'VE MADE THEM.

HOW DID THIS HAPPEN?

FIRST ARIA, NOW THIS. THE MORE THAT HAPPENS, THE MORE QUESTIONS I HAVE FOR DIANA.

WHO
ARE YOU?
WHY ARE
YOU DOING
THIS TO
ME?!

BECAUSE
YOU'RE A WITCH,
OF COURSE.

W-WAIT!
I'M NOT A
REGULAR
WITCH--
I'M WITH THE
WHs!!

WHs?

Y-YEAH. I'M NOT EVIL, I'M ON THE HUMANS' SIDE!

ZI POINT

SO WHAT? YOU'RE STILL A WITCH.

BANG

STEP

MASTER, I'VE DISPOSED OF HER SUPPORTER.

GOOD JOB...

HALLOWEEN.

TA! TUM

PEOPLE WHO LIKE TASHA

THE SHY ONES.

THE OUTGOING ONES.

HOW-EVER...

WHAT THE HELL? YOU'RE ALL AS **FLAT** AS THE WALL! NO WONDER TASHA HAS NO INTEREST IN GIRLS.

SHOCK

THOSE WERE XING'S FINAL RECORDED WORDS. HE WAS NEVER SEEN AGAIN.

11. THE SECRET GARDEN

I KNOW THIS WAS **GRAY** WHEN I FIRST GOT IT!

BUT ALL OF A SUDDEN, IT TURNED **BLACK!**

WOW, AMAZING.

THE UNIFORM HAS DETERMINED THAT YOU'RE A **BLACK** CLASS.

THE UNIFORM DID WHAT...?

OH, TASHA DIDN'T TELL YOU?

No, ma'am.

WH UNIFORMS CAN **MEASURE** OUR LEVEL OF COMPETENCY. THEY ASSIGN US OUR CLASS.

S-CLASS IS WHITE, A-CLASS IS BLACK, B-CLASS IS BLUE. THOSE ARE THE BATTLE CLASSES...

C-CLASS IS GREEN--THEY'RE NON-COMBAT, INVESTIGATION, AND NAVIGATION. AND FINALLY, GRAY D-CLASS DOES CLERICAL WORK. THE UNIFORM CHANGES COLOR ACCORDING TO EACH PERSON'S ABILITY.

AND THAT'S JUST A TINY PIECE OF WHAT THESE UNIFORMS CAN DO.

WHOA, THAT INCREDIBLE

HONESTLY, I THINK *YOU'RE* THE INCREDIBLE ONE.

THE UNIFORM ACKNOWLEDGED YOU AS A BLACK CLASS THE FIRST TIME YOU PUT IT ON...

HECK, EVEN I WAS A BLUE CLASS MY FIRST TIME.

A WITCH WITH A SUPPORTER OF COMMONERS...

IS TRULY AN AMAZING THING.

UM, MAY I ASK A QUESTION?

SURE, WHAT IS IT?

UH, WHAT EXACTLY IS A "SUPPORTER OF COMMONERS"? ACTUALLY, WHAT'S A SUPPORTER? EVERYBODY KEEPS SAYING I HAVE ONE, BUT I DON'T KNOW WHAT IT MEANS.

DON'T WORRY-- EXPLAINING THIS STUFF IS PART OF MY JOB AS YOUR TEACHER.

OKAY, FIRST...

IT'S HER SERVANT, AND HER GUARDIAN.

WITCHES CAN USE THEIR SUPPORTERS TO MAGNIFY A SMALL PORTION OF THEIR MAGIC POWER BY THOUSANDS.

WHIRRRR

A WITCH'S SUPPORTER IS HER MOST **IMPORTANT** ASSET.

YOU COULD SAY THAT A WITCH IS ONLY AS STRONG AS HER SUPPORTER.

NOT ALL WITCHES EVEN *HAVE* SUPPORTERS, THOUGH.

GAINING A SUPPORTER IS VERY DIFFICULT, ACTUALLY. A WITCH HAS TO MEET MANY **CONDITIONS** TO GET ONE.

FIRST, SHE HAS TO FIND A SUPPORTER THAT HAS A **USEFUL** ABILITY OR SKILL, BUT THAT DOESN'T REQUIRE *MORE* MAGIC POWER THAN SHE HAS. PLUS, THE WITCH AND SUPPORTER NEED TO BE COMPATIBLE.

THE FINAL PART IS PROBABLY THE MOST IMPORTANT-- **THE WITCH'S WILL.**

MOST OF THE TIME, A WITCH HAS TO GO OUT AND **FIND** A SUPPORTER THAT MEETS ALL THOSE REQUIREMENTS.

BUT THERE'S ONE EXCEPTION--ONE TYPE OF SUPPORTER THAT BYPASSES THE WHOLE PROCESS.

YOUR SUPPORTER...

THU-THUM

A SUPPORTER OF COMMONERS.

YOUR SPIRITUAL SUPPORTER WAS BORN **DESTINED** FOR YOU.

YOUR LIFE IS THE SUPPORTER'S LIFE, AND YOUR DEATH IS ITS DEATH. IT CAN NEVER SERVE ANYONE BUT YOU.

A SUPPORTER OF COMMONERS IS BORN ON THE SAME DAY AS ITS MASTER, WITH AN UNBREAKABLE BOND ALREADY IN PLACE BETWEEN THEM.

AND THERE'S SO MUCH MORE TO IT THAN THAT. THEY HAVE **A TON OF** UNIQUE ABILITIES.

WOOOW...

WELL, THE FIRST BIG ADVANTAGE IS THAT THERE'S NO LEARNING PERIOD WHERE YOU AND YOUR SUPPORTER ARE ADAPTING TO EACH OTHER. PLUS, THE SPIRITUAL SUPPORTER HARDLY NEEDS ANY OF YOUR MANA TO FUNCTION.

CLINK

AND BEST OF ALL, YOUR SUPPORTER GENUINELY **CARES** ABOUT YOU AND **WANTS** TO PROTECT YOU.

THAT'S WHERE THEIR SPECIAL CHARACTERISTICS COME FROM.

OKAY, I'M DONE INFUSING MY MANA.

VMMM

THIS ARROW'S DESTRUCTIVE POWER WILL BE MULTIPLIED BY THOUSANDS.

KREEEEK

WHATEVER YOU DO, DON'T MISS. WE SENT TWO SQUADS AS BAIT...

DON'T WORRY. MY ACCURACY CAN MATCH THE MANA GUN MARKSMAN'S.

TURN

BOOM

어

MISS ARIA'S SPIRITUAL SUPPORTERS CAN DEFEND AND ATTACK AUTOMATICALLY...

BUT THERE ARE STILL **LIMITS** TO WHAT THEY CAN HANDLE.

YOUR TROOPS WERE PERFECT AS A PRACTICE RUN. ARIA'S SUPPORTERS ARE NEWLY HATCHED, SO THEY NEEDED TO GET A *FEEL* FOR HER POWERS.

SHUNK

AAAH!

WH-WHAT
IS THIS?!

AAAAAH!!

HOWEVER,
YOU'VE REACHED
THE END OF YOUR
USEFULNESS.
DISAPPEAR.

HM. IT'S QUIET...
SHE MUST HAVE
FINISHED.

ALL THAT'S LEFT IS FOR HIM TO TAKE THE BAIT...

DIANA, COULD YOU TAKE A LOOK AT THIS?

MY, MY... YOU STILL HAVE THE ENERGY LEFT TO MOVE? AMAZING.

IT'S AN ACCESSORY OFF THE CLOTHES OF A WITCH I FOUGHT RECENTLY.

WITCHES CREATE THEIR OWN CLOTHING AND ACCESSORIES.

I'M SURE YOU CAN TRACK DOWN THE SOURCE OF THE MAGIC, NO PROBLEM.

BUT FIRST...

DO YOU REALLY HAVE TO TAKE THAT FORM?

YOU LOOK JUST LIKE ARIA, AND YOU'RE EVEN SITTING IN HER OLD BEDROOM... IT'S MAKING ME SERIOUSLY UNCOMFORTABLE.

THERE'S NOTHING I CAN DO, TASHA GODSPELL.

THE ABILITY TO SHOW MY OPPONENT THE THING HE MOST WANTS TO SEE...

AND TO HIDE BOTH MYSELF AND MY SUPPORTER WITHIN THAT ILLUSION...

WHAT WAS
THAT...? IT FELT
LIKE SOMEONE
RUMMAGING
AROUND IN MY
BRAIN...

Giggle

HUH?

IN RETURN, I'LL OFFER YOU...

BA-

BMP

ACCESS TO MY BOUNDLESS INFORMATION.

JUST THINK ABOUT IT. IT'S NOT A BAD DEAL--IF YOU JUST LET ME PLACE THIS TINY MAGICAL LINE INSIDE YOU, YOU'LL GAIN ACCESS TO ALL THE INFORMATION YOU DESIRE.

I DON'T KNOW... IF SHE DOES THIS, I'LL COMPLETELY LOSE MY PRIVACY...

FOR EXAMPLE

A LIST OF THE WORLD'S WEALTHIEST PEOPLE, RATED BY GULLIBILITY.

SWISH

SWISH

Whoa...

Whee!

GOTCHA!

GRAB

YOINK

AT THE CK **WAS** THAT?

HEE HEE...

TASHA, IT LOOKS LIKE YOUR PATH WILL BE EVEN *MORE* UNEXPECTED THAN I FIRST THOUGHT.

Giggle

Giggle

SHE MANAGED TO ESCAPE FROM MY INFORMATION RADAR. SHE'S A FORCE TO BE **RECKONED** WITH.

DID IT FAIL?

ARE YOU SERIOUS? I DON'T JUST *FAIL*.

IF YOU COMPLETE YOUR NEXT MISSION, I'LL GIVE YOU YOUR ANSWER WHEN YOU GET BACK.

WHAT MISSION?

OH, YOU'LL HEAR ABOUT IT SOON ENOUGH.

AH, THERE IT IS...

BE
BE
BEE

FLIP

POP

EMERGENCY BROADCAST

All WH battle classes:
A HELP request has been received.
Please report to the briefing room immediately.

GET GOING! YOU NEED ALL THE WITCHES' HATS YOU CAN GET, RIGHT?

I'LL TAKE CARE OF YOUR PROBATION.

YOU KNEW THIS WOUL HAPPEN...? YOU WEREN KIDDING ABOUT BEIN MASTER OF THE NETWORK.

TURN

WA
HO
O

HUH?

BECAUSE THE ONLY THING THAT BLOCKS ME FROM SEEING SOMEONE'S FUTURE...

IS WHEN THE **FOUR GREAT WITCHES** GET INVOLVED.

AT LAST...

WE FOUND THE WITCHES' CASTLE!

EVEN AGAINST A WITCH YOU'D USUALLY BEAT EASILY, IF YOU'RE FIGHTING IN HER OWN CASTLE...

IT'LL TAKE AT LEAST **TWO** TEAMS OF A-CLASS WHs TO GUARANTEE VICTORY.

BOOM

HUH...?

BOOM

투 KA-캉 콩

BROOSH 콩

WHAT THE HECK'S GOING ON?!

I DON'T KNOW! WE'D BETTER CHECK IT OUT!

OPTION

ARIA'S SUPPORTER "AEGIS" CAN AUTOMATICALLY ATTACK AND DEFEND.

AND ITS BONUS FEATURE...

PRESS

I THINK WE NEED SOME NEW FIGHT MUSIC TODAY.

CLICK

CD PLAYER OPTION ?!!

WE'VE MANAGED TO **UPGRADE** YOUR GEAR USING THE BOOKS LADY FLORENCE LEFT US.

OL.

FIRST, YOUR NEW UNIFORM.

BUT MORE IMPORTANTLY...

THE DIMENSIONAL POUCH WAS MERELY A PRACTICE TOOL. IT'S BEEN UPGRADED TO **GLOVE FORM.**

WHAT?!

THIS GLOVE IS THE **REAL** FORM OF MY DIMENSIONAL GALLERY POUCH?!

ITS DEFENSIVE CAPABILITIES HAVE BEEN **GREATLY** IMPROVED--YOUR OLD ONE DOESN'T COMPARE. IT ALSO **WON'T** RESTRICT YOUR MOVEMENT.

THAT'S WHAT THE BOOK SAID.

AREN'T YOU SUPPOSED TO BE ON *PROBATION?*

OH MY, MR. KUNEIN! MR. WORTH!

GREAT, IT'S THE JERK BRIGADE.

YOU'RE NOT SUPPOSED TO BE HERE, TASHA.

YOU SHOULD BE LOCKED AWAY SOMEWHERE, LIKE THE CRIMINAL YOU ARE.

THROW AWAY THE KEY! MWA HA HA HA!

LINDA?

YES.

HERE YOU ARE, MR. KUNEIN.

Huh?

MONEY, AND...
(LOUD)

POWERFUL FRIENDS!!
(EVEN LOUDER)

GETTING A LETTER LIKE THIS IS CHILD'S PLAY NOW THAT **DIANA'S** GOT MY BACK... HA HA HA!

N-NO...!

TP TP

I CAN'T ACCEPT THIS!

SULK SULK SULK

HEH HEH... SILLY KID, YOU NEED TO *GROW UP* BEFORE YOU CAN PLAY WITH THE *BIG BOYS.*

12. THE SEAL

WHO THE HECK ARE YOU?!

SHOVE

SLIDE

HEY, THAT'S *MY* LINE!

ARE YOU... THE REAL HALLOWEEN?

UGH. RAN, THAT'S CRAPPY! YOU REALLY COULDN'T TELL ME APART FROM THAT *FAKE*? OH, HEY, BAGHEERA, YOU'RE ALL BASHED UP!

Ooh, I know that attitude anywhere.

It appears you've figured it out.

IF HALLOWEEN'S HERE, THEN THAT MEANS...!

GOOD, I'M NOT TOO LATE.

TMP

IT'S FINALLY JUST THE TWO OF US.

THAT'S A MANA GUN, RIGHT? **WHERE** DID YOU GET IT?

BUT BEFORE WE GET STARTED, I HAVE A FEW QUESTIONS.

AND ALL THE RECENT **MURDERS** OF WITCHES AND WITCH HUNTERS... WAS THAT YOU?

ALL THOSE QUESTIONS...

TODAY, I'LL TEACH YOU HOW TO **DODGE** A MANA GUN BULLET.

WHY WOULD I BOTHER LEARNING *THAT?* NO ONE ELSE CAN SHOOT THIS GUN.

HEY, MORON. IF YOU CAN DODGE THE FASTEST BULLET DODGING ANY *OTHE* LONG-RANGE WEAPC WILL BE A BREEZE.

IT'S EASY. WHEN I PULL THE TRIGGER, IT TAKES LESS THAN A TENTH OF A SECOND FOR THE BULLET REACH YOU.

BUT HOW DO YOU DODGE SOMETHING YOU CAN'T EVEN SEE?

DURING THAT TIME...

JUST MAKE SURE YOU'RE NOT IN THE MANA GUN'S LINE OF FIRE.

NORMAL HUMAN REACTION TIME IS SOMEWHERE BETWEEN 0.1 AND 0.15 SECONDS.

BUT WITH *INTENSIVE TRAINING,* WE CAN BRING IT DOWN TO 0.03 SECONDS.

BANG

FWOOSH

KrK

UH?

I SEE YOU'VE MASTERED THE ART OF DODGING BULLETS MID-FIRE.

CRNCH

CRNCH

WHAT ?

THEN...

TWIRL

TAK

HOW ABOUT THIS?

WELL...

CREAK

CRACK

THERE'S NO DOUBT ABOUT IT.

I'M STRONGER THAN YOU.

AND MY SUPPORTER...

IS ALSO STRONGER THAN YOURS.

DA

DUUM

MASTER? CAN I KILL HIM? CAN I?!

HALLO-WEEN!!

WOOSH

!!

BANG

HE MISSED ON PURPOSE...

WOOOSH

WATCH IT, HALLOWEEN!!

BOOK-4

13. POWER AND SPEED

YOUR SUPPORTER IS GOING TO DIE.

AND ONCE YOU LOSE, YOU'LL ANSWER MY QUESTIONS.

NOT...

GONNA..

GOT ONE
SHOT. I'
MAKE I
COUNT.

restoration of the truth

POINT

I WON'T LET
HALLOWEEN
DIE.

POP

STARTING TODAY, YOU'RE OFFICIALLY AN **AGENT** OF THE WH WESTERN DISTRICT CENTER!

TEE HEE HEE...

DON'T WORRY, YOU'RE MY STUDENT. YOU'LL QUALIFY AS A B-CLASS **WH** AT LEAST, NO PROBLEM.

I GUARANTEE IT!

SO?

BIG SURPRISE, RIGHT? I BET YOU DIDN'T THINK YOU'D MAKE IT IN ONLY A YEAR!

SO GO, AND LEARN **EVERYTHING** YOU CAN!

YES, MA'AM.

MY TEACHER...

YOU'LL STAY AT THE CENTER DURING YOUR TRAINING PERIOD. I'M NOT SURE HOW LONG THAT'LL BE, THOUGH.

A FEW DAYS BEFORE I WAS ACCEPTED AS A WH...

I GUESS THIS IS GOODBYE, FOR NOW.

IN A BATTLE AGAINST MY YOUNGER SISTER, ARIA...

OH YEAH, I HAVE A PRESENT FOR YOU.

SHE DIED.

IN HONOR OF YOUR GRADUATION.

THEY SAID HE WAS SO POWERFUL, AND SO DANGEROUS, THAT IT TOOK **TWO SEALS** TO KEEP HIM UNDER CONTROL.

THE SEALS WEAKEN HIM. THEY LOCK AWAY HIS TRUE FORM AND MEMORIES. BUT DESPITE ALL THAT, HE'S STILL VERY STRONG.

MY TEACHER WARNED ME NOT TO BREAK THE SEALS-- SHE SAID IT WOULD BE TOO DANGEROUS.

BUT I DON'T WANT TO LOSE THE GIFT SHE GAVE ME!

I WON'T LOSE MY SUPPORTER!

SO...

I BROKE THE FIRST SEAL.

IS THIS REALLY IT? THE SUPPORTER THAT CAN'T BE CONTROLLED WITHOUT TWO MAGIC SEALS?

MY SUPPORTER'S TRUE FORM AND STRENGTH...

WHEW...

HUH?!

UH... HALLOW-EEN?

SPIN

Ack?!

BA-BOOM! FVO

TUMBLE

SLAM

CRASH

Yay~!♪

SPARKLE

THROWING A REAL PUNCH... FEELS SO GOOD! ♡

I'M OVER FLOWING WITH POWER!

THE HECK WAS **THAT**, HALLOWEEN? ARE YOU **TRYING** TO KILL ME?!

TURN

HEH... I SEE YOU'RE STILL ALIVE.

GOOD, GOOD. IT'LL TAKE MORE THAN **ONE** MEASLY PUNCH TO GET OUT ALL MY STORED RESENTMENT.

CRAP!

K-KRACK

H-HANG ON... TIME OUT...

I THOUGHT YOU WERE GONNA DESTROY ME.

HOW'S HE DOING THAT?!

HE'S DODGING ALL MY ATTACKS!

I KNOW I'M FASTER AND MORE POWERFUL--THIS SHOULD BE *EASY!*

WIFF

JUST HIT ALREADY!

KLANG

THROW

KYAA ?!

CRASH TUMBI BAM SLAM

UGH!

YOU LOOK SURPRISED.

YOU MUST BE WONDERING WHY YOU CAN'T WIN AGAINST ME, DESPITE YOUR SUPERIOR STRENGTH AND SPEED.

I GUESS THAT MAKES SENSE. I *DID* CANCEL YOUR FULL-POWER ATTACK, AFTER ALL.

THERE'S ONE SIMPLE REASON...

YOU HAVE NO *SKILL*.

HEY!

YOU SWING YOUR SWORDS WILDLY, WITH NO CONTROL. IT'S SIMPLE TO READ YOUR SLOPPY ATTACKS.

NICE DODGING.

TMP

YOU HAVE EYES IN THE BACK OF YOUR HEAD?

EXPLAIN YOURSELF, TASHA! YOU NEARLY KILLED ME!

CALM DOWN... YOU SURVIVED, RIGHT?

WOOSH

IT'S NOT LIKE YOU HAVEN'T TRIED TO KILL *ME* BEFORE. LET'S JUST SAY WE'RE EVEN...

HMPH!

WHERE'RE YOU GOING?

TURN

I NEED TO SETTLE THINGS WITH THIS GUY.

AS LONG AS THE SECOND SEAL IS STILL IN PLACE, YOU'RE MY SUPPORTER.

I'LL HAVE TO USE MY MANA TO KEEP YOU UNDER CONTROL NOW.

CRUD! HOW CAN HE CONTROL ME WITH SO LITTLE MANA? I DIDN'T THINK HE COULD!

NOW THAT WE'VE WORKED THAT OUT...

LET'S GIVE IT ANOTHER TRY!

I'M OUT OF TIME...

HALLOWEEN HAS BEEN GETTING WEAKER AND WEAKER.

THE DAMAGE TO HIS HEART MUST BE WORSE THAN I THOUGHT. I NEED TO TREAT IT QUICKLY...

DEFEATING THESE TWO SHOULDN'T BE DIFFICULT...

BUT CAN HALLOWEEN HOLD ON UNTIL THEN...?

I GUESS HAVE NO CHOICE.

NO WAY! HE'S RELEASING HIS LIMITERS?!

A MALE HUMAN SHOULDN'T BE ABLE TO DO THAT!

NOW.

DA

DUUN

COME AT
ME.

FLICK

I'LL SHOW
YOU THE
TRUE POWER
OF THE
DIMENSIONAL
GALLERY!

RIVAL [1]

FELICE FIDELIER, ASSIGNED TO COOGA.

THE CENTER CLASSIFIES MR. COOGA'S RELATIONSHIP WITH MR. TASHA AS A RIVALRY...

WHAT DO YOU THINK?

HA! THAT LOSER TASHA?

THEY THINK HE'S MY RIVAL? THAT'S FREAKIN' HILARIOUS. ANYWAY, DO THIS FOR ME.

A NEW UNIFORM REQUEST?

I DON'T WASTE MY TIME THINKING ABOUT SOMEBODY THAT FAR BENEATH ME.

SHOES

Shoes must be 6cm taller than Tasha's shoes.

RIGHT... YOU DON'T CARE ABOUT HIM AT ALL...

THEY'RE ALL...

DEAD...

I'M ALL ALONE...

LOOKS LIKE
YOU'RE THE LAST
ONE STANDING.

BRAVE WORDS.

BUT CAN YOU DEFEAT MY FAMILIARS?

WHAT THE HECK IS THIS?

I'M SURE I ALREADY KILLED THEM!

INFINITE FAMILIARS.

I'VE KNOWN FOR A WHILE NOW THAT I WAS UNDER SURVEILLANCE.

THAT'S WHY I AVOIDED USING ALL OF MY SUPPORTER'S ABILITIES.

ESPECIALLY ITS GREATEST ABILITY...

PURPOSELY THROWING HER LIFE AWAY.

IT'S TOO BAD.

FINDING A STUDENT IS TURNING OUT TO BE DIFFICULT.

HEY THERE, GORGEOUS~!

SHHHHSsssssss

M-MY FAMILIARS...

ALL DESTROYED ?!!

TMP

HEY, XING!

WHAT'S WRONG WITH HER?

OH, I GUESS SHE FAINTED. THE SUDDEN DESTRUCTION OF HER SUPPORTER MUST'VE HIT HER PRETTY HARD.

GOOD. NOW, HURRY AND TRANSFER HER SO WE CAN GET OUT OF HERE.

UGH, WHY IS A GREAT WH LIKE ME STUCK DOING THESE CRAPPY MISSIONS? THIS ISN'T EVEN WITCH HUNTING.

I KNOW I HAVE TO TRANSFER HER, YOU CAN KEEP YOUR IDIOTIC COMMENTS TO YOURSELF.

IF IT WEREN'T FOR THE ORDERS FROM WHITE CLASS WH VIHYUNGRANG, NOBODY WOULD EVER TEAM UP WITH YOU.

WHAT WAS THAT?!

A GUY LIKE YOU SHOULD BE HONORED TO TEAM UP WITH SOMEONE AS GLORIOUS AS ME!

WHAT'S SO GREAT ABOUT TEAMING UP WITH ANOTHER GUY?

And not even Tasha...

INCREDIBLE...

THIS IS THE POWER OF THE BLACK A-CLASS.

AN OPPONENT WE COULDN'T TOUCH, EVEN WHEN OUR LIVES DEPENDED ON IT...

BUT THEY DEFEATED HER SO EASILY!

I WORKED SO HARD TO BECOME A B-CLASS WH...

AND I WATCHED MY COMRADES DIE, BECAUSE IT WASN'T ENOUGH.

I FEEL SO STUPID.

ELMAR HYACINTH.

OF COURSE I KNOW YOU.

OUR MISSION HERE...

YOU... YOU KNOW MY NAME?

MAYBE YOU DIDN'T KNOW, BUT I HAVE EXTREMELY GOOD LUCK.

HEH...

WE'VE BARELY EVEN STARTED.

ALL RIGHT ...

THEN LET ME ASK YOU SOMETHING.

WHY ARE YOU TRYING TO STOP ME? THE WITCHES ARE THE ONES WHO MURDERED OUR TEACHER!

I GUESS THAT'S TECHNICALLY TRUE.

I WAS EXPELLED.

BUT THAT DOESN'T CHANGE HOW I FEEL ABOUT OUR TEACHER. I STILL RESPECT HER AS MUCH AS EVER.

THAT'S WHY I CAN NEVER FORGIVE THEM.

THE ONES WHO *KILLED* OUR TEACHER...

THE WITCHES!!

I DON'T KNOW MUCH YET, ONLY THAT THE MURDERER IS **DEFINITELY** A WITCH.

AND IF SHE WAS ABLE TO BEAT OUR TEACHER, I PROBABLY CAN'T DEFEAT HER AT MY CURRENT STRENGTH.

FFFSSSSSSS

I HUNT WITCHES TO **ABSORB** THEIR MANA AND MAKE MYSELF STRONGER.

BUT...WHY DO YOU **KILL THEM?!** IF YOU WANT THEIR MANA, ALL YOU NEED IS THEIR **HATS!!**

OUR TEACHER WAS **MURDERED** BY A WITCH.

THERE'S NO WAY TO KNOW IF A WITCH I DEFEAT IS THE KILLER...

ONCE I REALIZED THAT, I COULDN'T LET A SINGLE ONE LIVE.

THAT'S YOUR REASON?! THAT'S THE DUMBEST THING I'VE EVER HEARD!!

IT'S THE ONLY WAY TO BE SURE!

EVEN THOUGH WE SHARED A TEACHER, IF YOU KEEP INTERFERING WITH MY BUSINESS, I **WON'T** HESITATE TO KILL YOU.

SHOCK

THIS GUY IS DANGEROUS!

WAY TOO DANGEROUS...

IF I DON'T STOP HIM, RAN WILL BE IN DANGER...

AND...ARIA. I HAVE TO BEAT HIM!

BUT, RIGHT NOW... I DON'T THINK I CAN.

THERE'S ONLY ONE WAY... I DON'T HAVE A CHOICE!

OPEN, DIMENSIONAL GALLERY!

FLEX

GIVE ME... MOIRAE'S--

I WOULDN'T DO THAT IF I WERE YOU.

TP

WHO ARE YOU?

JUST THINK OF ME AS A FRIENDLY MEDDLER.

INTERESTING.

NOW...

SAY YOUR FAREWELLS.

YOU THINK YOU CAN BEAT ME?

WOOSH

TH- THAT'S...!

THE GIANT WHO SCORCHED THE EARTH, RULER OF MUSPELHEIM...

SURTR!!

YOU EVEN REMEMBERED THE NAME OF THE LAND SURTR RULED 5,000 YEARS AGO. YOUR TEACHER TAUGHT YOU WELL...

TEE HEE.

NOT BAD.

RYUHWAN.

SENSITIVE

KROOM

I GUESS I'LL HAVE TO FORCE YOU TO LISTEN, THEN.

SSS

HHHHS

SSS

IF THAT'S REALLY EAST'S SUPPORTER...

THEN I KNOW I DON'T HAVE A CHANCE.

BUT I WON'T HESITATE.

RRRSSHHH

HM...

IT DIDN'T WORK.

I MADE A LITTLE PROGRESS, THOUGH.

I MANAGED TO WOUND HIS STEEL-LIKE SKIN, JUST A LITTLE.

DRIPPP

I'LL WAIT FOR MY CHANCE, AND CONCENTRATE ALL MY POWER ON THAT SPOT...

STARE

BA-DMP

DRIP

DRIP

DRIP

LOOKS LIKE THE BACKLASH IS STARTING.

I THOUGHT SO.

EVEN FOR A FIGHTER LIKE YOU, WHEN YOU RELEASE THE LIMITERS ON YOUR MANA YOUR BODY WILL SUFFER FOR IT. I GUESS YOU WON'T BE ABLE TO USE ANY MANA FOR A WHILE.

AND...

THAT MEANS THIS GUY'S USELESS FOR NOW, TOO.

HALLOWEEN!!

YOUR SUPPORTER AND YOUR MANA...

YOU'VE MADE YOURSELF SO EASY TO KILL.

WITHOUT EITHER, WHATEVER WILL YOU DO?

RYUHWAN.

WHY...?

I DON'T UNDERSTAND THIS.

SHE SUDDENLY APPEARED...

AND JUST... ATTACKED THAT GUY.

UGH, PEOPLE LIKE YOU ALWAYS TRY THIS...

THEY DO SOMETHING NOBODY ASKED THEM TO, THEN DEMAND COMPENSATION.

YOU'RE THE *LAST* PERSON I WANT TO HEAR THAT LECTURE FROM.

YOU REALLY...

WANT THIS THING THAT BADLY?

OH, WHAT SHOULD I DO?

WH-WHAT DID YOU DO?!

A WITCH'S HAT APPEARS THE MOMENT SHE **AWAKENS** AS A WITCH. HER HAT IS HER MOST IMPORTANT POSSESSION, MORE **PRECIOUS** THAN HER LIFE.

SINCE WITCHES CAN ONLY HOLD SO MUCH MANA IN THEIR BODIES, THEY USE THEIR **HATS** TO STORE THE EXCESS MANA THEY CREATE. THEY USE IT AS A VITAL POWER SOURCE.

IF THE HAT IS DESTROYED, ALL THE **MANA** THE WITCH STORED OVER HER LIFETIME ALSO DISAPPEARS...

AND SHE JUST BLEW IT UP?!

DON'T FREAK OUT--THAT HAT WAS A **FAKE**.

WHAT?!

FOR SOME REASON...

SHHK

IF I BREAK THE SECOND SEAL, MY **CONTRACT** WITH HALLOWEEN IS OVER.

I WOULD NEVER DO THAT. NEVER!

BUT I'M NEVER GOING TO DO THAT, NO MATTER WHAT.

TEE HEE... YOU DON'T KNOW ANYTHING ABOUT YOUR SUPPORTER, DO YOU?

I'M TRYING TO TELL YOU-- YOUR SUPPORTER HAS THE POTENTIAL TO BECOME MUCH *STRONGER* IN HER CURRENT STATE.

!!

WELL, THEN.

FLOAT

I HOPE YOU **GROW** A LOT BEFORE WE MEET AGAIN, TASHA.

EVERYTHING ABOUT THIS PLACE...

LOOKS FAMILIAR TO ME.

I KNOW THAT I'M DREAMING... I'M SURE OF IT...

BECAUSE...

VARETE IS HERE BESIDE ME...

SO, EVERYONE ELSE WAS WELL ENOUGH TO RETURN TO THEIR ROOMS AFTER BEING TREATED?

KA-TUNK

KA-TUNK

I TREATED YOUR PHYSICAL WOUNDS, BUT I COULDN'T HEAL THE **MAGICAL** ONES

I'M SO SORRY.

IT'S BECAUSE I'M NOT SKILLED ENOUGH...

DON'T APOLOGIZE. I'M NOT IN ANY PAIN THANKS TO YOU, MS. HYACINTH.

PLEASE, JUST CALL ME ELMAR.

I'M NOT SURE IF THERE WILL BE ANY COMPLICA-TIONS. JUST REST FOR NOW, AND CALL ME IF YOU NEED ANYTHING.

BYE.

THUNK

POFF

I THOUGHT I WAS STRONGER THAN THAT.

UP, UNTIL NOW...

I'VE FOUGHT COUNTLESS WITCHES, AND I'VE BEEN IN TOUGH SPOTS BEFORE, BUT I NEVER ACTUALLY FELT WEAK!

I THOUGHT I'D BE ABLE TO SAVE ARIA SOON.

I OVERESTIMATED MYSELF.

I HATE IT!
I HATE
BEING
WEAK!

HOW MUCH
STRONGER
DO I HAVE
TO GET TO
REACH
YOU?

ARIA...!

CRAP!

I'M SO PISSED OFF, I CAN'T STAY *QUIET* ANYMORE! THIS IS A CONFERENCE OF HIGH RANKING WITCHES!

SO, WHY ARE THESE TWO *HUMANS* HERE?!

CALM DOWN, ROSE. THEY'RE ONLY SUPPORTERS.

BANG

SUPPORTERS OR NOT, I HATE ALL HUMANS! WHO'S THEIR OWNER?!

THEY DO NOT HAVE MASTERS.

IT APPEARS ALL OUR MEMBERS HAVE ARRIVED. SHALL WE BEGIN?

WE NEED TO DISCUSS...

THE SECOND WAR AGAINST HUMANITY.

WHILE YOU WERE SLEEPING

JUST AS I THOUGHT.

THE KING IS MOVING AS I PREDICTED.

WELL, IT'S SURPRISING THAT **SOUTH** HAS STAYED QUIET THIS LONG. THEY CALL HER THE "KING OF CONFLICT," AFTER ALL.

IT'S GOING TO GET **NOISY** VERY SOON.

16. THE CONTRACT OF DESTRUCTION

HEY,
COOGA...

WHAT?
DID I SAY
ANYTHING THA'
WASN'T TRUE?

NO, IT'S NOT THAT..
I WAS JUST
WONDERING WHY
WE'RE SEEING EYE
TO-EYE ALL OF A
SUDDEN.

YOU SHOULD
BE 6CM
SHORTER.

HOW
HUMILIATING...

WH-WHY ARE
YOU CHANGING THE
SUBJECT?!

AHA!

LOOKS LIKE YOU GOT YOURSELF SOME *MAGIC SHOES* (A.K.A. HIGH HEELS).

MY SHOES MAKE ME 3CM TALLER, SO YOURS MUST BE...9CM?

I UNDERSTAND THAT YOU'RE SHORT, BUT 9CM? EVEN WITCHES ONLY GO 8CM MAX...

TH-THAT DOESN'T MATTER! AND I'M STILL *GROWING!!*

OOH, STILL GROWING, HUH?

SHHK

IN THE PAST TWO YEARS I'VE GROWN 5CM...AND YOU...

DON'T-- DON'T SAY IT!

0.5CM...

SMM!!

That's pretty bad.

His soul is leaving.

STOP RIGHT THERE!!

He came back to life?!

I TOLD YOU TO *STOP*, YOU STUPID JERK!

CHEAT! *LIAR!* DON'T TAKE ANOTHER STEP!!

ARE YOU DEAF?! YOU WHITE-HAIRED *MORON!!*

AW, CRAP.

BANG

TAKE IT EASY, TASHA.

DON'T INTERFERE, XING.

THOSE ARE REAL BULLETS... YOU DON'T WANT TO *KILL* HIM.

THIS PUNK JUST INSULTED MY TEACHER. MY WHITE HAIR IS PROOF THAT I WAS THE STUDENT OF EDEA FLORENCE.

EVEN IF IT'S JUST A JOKE, I WON'T FORGIVE ANYONE WHO INSULTS IT.

YEAH, BUT--

BESIDES, I REPRESSED MOST OF THE MAGIC IN THAT BULLET. IT WOULD'VE BEEN REALLY PAINFUL, BUT HE WOULDN'T HAVE DIED.

HE'D PROBABLY JUST END UP IN THE HOSPITAL FOR A FEW DAYS... OR MONTHS.

SCARY.

I UNDER- STAND YOUR POINT AND ALL...

BUT YOU GO BERSERK WHENEVER ANYONE MENTIONS YOUR HAIR.

DO YOU THINK YOU COULD TONE IT DOWN A LITTLE?

BZZZ

THAT COWARDLY ATTACK....

IF YOU'D ONLY STAYED DOWN, I WOULD HAVE LET THIS GO...

WISH

FUNNY, WE FEEL THE SAME.

WISH

SWOOOH

THNK

WE HAVE TO STOP THEM...!

YOU'LL DIE IF YOU GET INVOLVED.

BUT--

EVEN AMONG THE A-CLASS, THOSE GUYS ARE THE ELITES.

THERE'S ONLY ONE PERSON WHO CAN STOP THEM...

SINCE
WHEN IS
THE
CENTER A
PLAY-
GROUND
FOR
CHILDREN
?

IF YOU *MUST* CONTINUE...

WOULD YOU ALLOW MY **LADIES** TO JOIN THE FUN?

PHANTOM KNIGHT!!

TURN

COOGA. WE'RE GOING.

WE'RE LEAVING TOO, HALLOWEEN.

TASHA, WAIT!

YOU NEED TO STOP GETTING INTO THESE FIGHTS AT THE CENTER.

EDEA PERSONALLY ASKED ME TO WATCH OVER YOU, SO HEED MY ADVICE.

I NEVER ASKED YOU TO.

THAT KID, WHY'S HE SO SENSITIVE TODAY?

HE'S BEEN IN A ROTTEN MOOD SINCE HE FAILED HIS MISSION.

OH, ARE YOU MISS HYACINTH?

Yes...

PLEASE COME WITH ME.

I'D LIKE TO SPEAK TO YOU IN MY OFFICE. XING, GO GET SOME REST.

UM...

IS THIS *REALLY A* SUPPORTER?

IT LOOKS LIKE A NORMAL SWORD HILT.

THIS MAGIC SWORD HAS TAKEN COUNT-LESS LIVES. DON'T BE FOOLED BY ITS APPEARANCE.

TO BE HONEST, I'M NOT SURE GIVING IT TO YOU IS THE RIGHT THING TO DO...

BUT WE DESPERATELY NEED MORE A-CLASS WHS RIGHT NOW, AND YOU ARE CURRENTLY THE **BEST** MATCH FOR IT.

HOWEVER, THE CHOICE IS ULTIMATELY YOURS...

MISS HYACINTH.

THE CHOICE IS YOURS...

FOOLISH CREATURE.

GRIP

I....

I WANT POWER!

GIVE ME YOUR STRENGTH, AND I'LL GIVE YOU MY BLOOD!

I KNOW WHAT IT'S LIKE TO BE WEAK.

I'VE STOOD BY, HELPLESS, AND WATCHED MY COMRADES DIE AROUND ME.

STARE

Tee hee...

WHAT, NO COMMENT? HEH HEH...

WE...
...

NUDGE

NUDGE

NUDGE

GOOD JOB, LINDA.

That's it.

I didn't mean for me...

BY THE WAY, SET UP A MEETING WITH DIANA FOR ME...

THE SOONER, THE BETTER.

SURE, THAT SHOULD BE EASY. YOU'RE A SPECIAL CASE NOW, SO IT'LL ONLY TAKE A FEW DAYS.

I'LL LEAVE IT TO YOU.

OKAY...

THAT WAS... AWKWARD. HE REALLY DOESN'T SEEM LIKE HIMSELF.

HANG ON, TASHA!

WH-WHERE'D THAT COME FROM?!

I'M BROKE! YOU CAN'T MOOCH OFF ME!

BEEP BEEP BEEP BEEP

A CALL?

BEEP BEEP BEEP BEEP BEEP

THE LIGHT'S RED...

AN URGENT MESSAGE!

WHAT IS IT?

I'VE NEVER GOTTEN A MESSAGE LIKE THIS BEFORE...

ALL WH'S MUST ABANDON THEIR CURRENT MISSIONS AND RETURN TO THE CENTER IMMEDIATELY. TOP PRIORITY.

WHIRRRRR

WHIRRR

IF IT CANNOT BE MINE...

THEN IT WILL BURN!

ARTHUR...

IF IT IS NOT A PLACE WHERE YOU RULE, I WILL SHOW NO MERCY...

BAIRONG EMPIRE!

UNTIL THE TOTAL *DESTRUCTION* OF BRITAIN.

CRASH

UGH...THIS IS INSANE...

HOW COULD THIS HAPPEN?

FFWO

OOO

ONE SINGLE WITCH, ALONE...

RIVAL [2]

EVERYONE'S TALKING ABOUT HOW YOU AND MR. COOGA ARE RIVALS. WHAT DO YOU THINK?

What?!

HE'S THE ONE MAKING A BIG DEAL OUT OF IT!

I'M ABOVE ALL THAT! I WOULD NEVER BOTHER DECLARING A GUY LIKE THAT MY RIVAL!

IF YOU REALLY DON'T CARE... WHY DID YOU MEMORIZE HIS HEIGHT CHANGES FOR THE LAST TWO YEARS?

AFTERMATH

DEFENDING MY RIGHT TO THE AFTERMATH!!

YO! HELLO, EVERYONE! I'M 'LOWEEN.

THANK YOU TO ALL THE READERS WHO BOUGHT THIS VOLUME!

THIS BOOK WAS MUCH TOO EVENTFUL.

WE INTRODUCED A BUNCH OF NEW CHARACTERS, WHICH MEANT MANY NEW CLOTHING DESIGNS, AND MANY MORE DEADLINES...

I WAS SURPRISED BY HOW POPULAR THE NEW CHARACTERS ALV AND COOGA ARE.

ESPECIALLY THIS GUY!

COMPARED TO HIM, THE NUMBER OF TIMES I APPEARED...

MAYBE I SHOULDN'T APPEAR AT ALL...

HOWEVER! YOUR ENCOURAGEMENTS GIVE ME STRENGTH! I WILL CONTINUE TO DEFEND MY RIGHT TO ANNOUNCE ALL THE END NOTES!

OKAY, OKAY. BACK TO THE POINT, I ALWAYS PLANNED TO DO A Q&A, BUT LOTS OF PEOPLE REQUESTED MORE CHARACTER DESCRIPTIONS SO I INCLUDED ANOTHER SET OF CHARACTER BIOS TOO.

CUTTY37 AND SONYARIO ASKED FOR THE CHARACTER BIOS. KORONG WANTS TO KNOW ABOUT THE DIFFERENT TYPES OF WHS. THANK YOU!

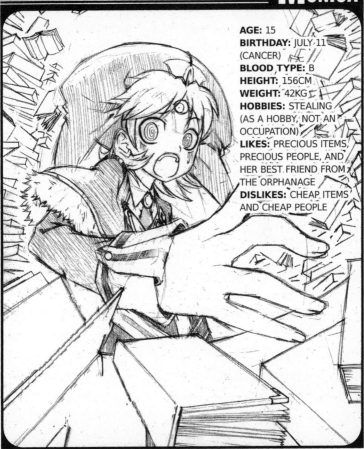

MONICA

AGE: 15
BIRTHDAY: JULY 11 (CANCER)
BLOOD TYPE: B
HEIGHT: 156CM
WEIGHT: 42KG
HOBBIES: STEALING (AS A HOBBY, NOT AN OCCUPATION)
LIKES: PRECIOUS ITEMS, PRECIOUS PEOPLE, AND HER BEST FRIEND FROM THE ORPHANAGE
DISLIKES: CHEAP ITEMS AND CHEAP PEOPLE

THE MONICA PICTURED HERE IS IN CRISIS. POOR MONICA, WHO'S NEVER BEEN TO SCHOOL BEFORE... HAS TO LEARN 15 YEARS WORTH OF CLASSWORK ALL AT ONCE. ^^; SINCE MONICA'S AN ORPHAN, SHE DOESN'T HAVE A LAST NAME. HER BIRTHDAY IS ONE SHE MADE UP WITH HER BEST FRIEND. SHE WAS ONE OF THE MAIN CHARACTERS THROUGH VOLUMES TWO AND THREE, BUT SHE'LL HAVE A TOUGH TIME APPEARING FROM NOW ON (BECAUSE SHE HAS A LOT OF STUDYING TO DO). I MADE HER EXTREMELY COMPATIBLE WITH TASHA, BUT IT LOOKS LIKE SHE WON'T GET TO HANG OUT WITH HIM ANYTIME SOON. ^^; ANYWAY, YOU'LL SEE HER AGAIN AT SOME POINT, BUT UNTIL THEN, BYE BYE!

WORDS DLONDY VON WWORTH

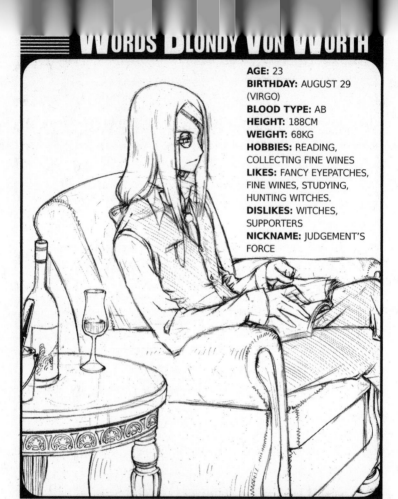

AGE: 23
BIRTHDAY: AUGUST 29 (VIRGO)
BLOOD TYPE: AB
HEIGHT: 188CM
WEIGHT: 68KG
HOBBIES: READING, COLLECTING FINE WINES
LIKES: FANCY EYEPATCHES, FINE WINES, STUDYING, HUNTING WITCHES.
DISLIKES: WITCHES, SUPPORTERS
NICKNAME: JUDGEMENT'S FORCE

NOBLE, FANCY, DIGNIFIED...HIS CHARACTER WAS CREATED WITH ALL THAT IN MIND. THIS IS HIS FIRST APPEARANCE (ORIGINALLY, TASHA WAS ALSO SUPPOSED TO BE OF NOBLE BLOOD, BUT HE WAS DEMOTED). STRANGELY, ALL THE WH MEMBERS SEEMED A BIT CHILDISH, SO I DECIDED I NEEDED SOMEONE MORE DIGNIFIED. THAT□S HOW I ENDED UP CREATING A MEMBER OF THE NOBILITY. PLUS, A CHARACTER WITH AN EYEPATCH IS AN ESSENTIAL PART OF EVERY COMIC (NOT TO MENTION SOMEBODY WITH GLASSES). ISN'T HE SEXY? ^^

THIS CHARACTER WAS MADE ALONGSIDE WORDS. HE'S THE COMPLETE OPPOSITE OF WORDS, BUT THEY GET ALONG VERY WELL (COOGA LOOKS UP TO HIM). HE STAYS WITH WORDS IN HIS LARGE, PRIVATE (EXPENSIVE) ROOM. ^^ THEY`RE ALSO TEAMMATES. TRUTH IS, COOGA AND WORDS WERE MADE TO DEMONSTRATE THAT THERE ARE WHs WHO HATE ALL WITCHES, EVEN THOSE WHO ARE SUPPOSED TO BE THEIR ALLIES.

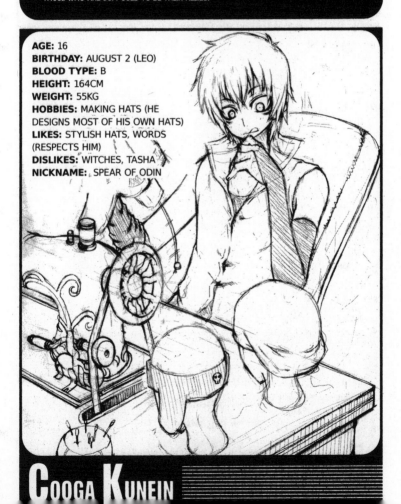

AGE: 16
BIRTHDAY: AUGUST 2 (LEO)
BLOOD TYPE: B
HEIGHT: 164CM
WEIGHT: 55KG
HOBBIES: MAKING HATS (HE DESIGNS MOST OF HIS OWN HATS)
LIKES: STYLISH HATS, WORDS (RESPECTS HIM)
DISLIKES: WITCHES, TASHA
NICKNAME: SPEAR OF ODIN

COOGA KUNEIN

ECLIPSE SHADENON

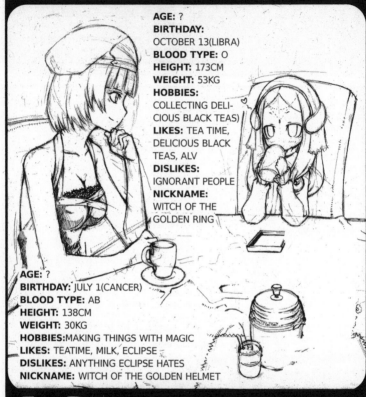

AGE: ?
BIRTHDAY:
OCTOBER 13(LIBRA)
BLOOD TYPE: O
HEIGHT: 173CM
WEIGHT: 53KG
HOBBIES:
COLLECTING DELI-
CIOUS BLACK TEAS)
LIKES: TEA TIME,
DELICIOUS BLACK
TEAS, ALV
DISLIKES:
IGNORANT PEOPLE
NICKNAME:
WITCH OF THE
GOLDEN RING

AGE: ?
BIRTHDAY: JULY 1(CANCER)
BLOOD TYPE: AB
HEIGHT: 138CM
WEIGHT: 30KG
HOBBIES: MAKING THINGS WITH MAGIC
LIKES: TEATIME, MILK, ECLIPSE
DISLIKES: ANYTHING ECLIPSE HATES
NICKNAME: WITCH OF THE GOLDEN HELMET

ALV BRONTE

HMM...THESE TWO WITCHES HAVE A PRETTY INVOLVED BACKSTORY. ECLIPSE TAKES CARE OF THE EMOTIONALLY UNSTABLE ALV (THERE'S A REASON FOR ALV'S INSTABILITY THAT I WON'T GO INTO HERE). I HOPE TO ONE DAY SHARE THE STORY OF HOW THEY MET. ^^ MANY TEAMS ARE SO CLOSE THAT THEY SHARE ROOMS; THESE TWO ARE ONE EXAMPLE. MORE OF THEIR STORY WILL BE REVEALED IN THE FUTURE, SO KEEP YOUR EYES PEELED!

THE DIFFERENT TYPES OF WITCH HUNTERS

KORONG ASKED IF DIFFERENT WITCH HUNTERS USE DIFFERENT TYPES OF MAGIC.
I'LL USE THIS SPACE TO DESCRIBE ANOTHER SUBDIVISION OF WITCH HUNTERS.
THEY CAN BE DIVIDED BOTH BY CLASS (OR LEVEL), AND ALSO BY THEIR TYPE OF MAGIC.
THERE ARE FIVE DIFFERENT TYPES: NATURAL, ESPER, SHAMAN, WITCH, AND MUTANT.

NATURAL

Natural WHs are normal human beings, however, through rigorous training, they are able to perform feats far beyond those of mortal men. Xing is an example. There are more Natural WHs than any other type, but the majority of them are in B-class. They make up the smallest portion of the A-class, and in the highest White class, which only has eight members in the entire world, there is only one.

ESPER

Espers are male supernaturals. In the Witch Hunter world, all girls are born with innate magic power, but only a few develop into witches. Similarly, Espers are boys who develop powerful supernatural abilities that may even rival the power of witches--
but they are far rarer than their female counterparts. Cooga is an example of an Esper.

SHAMAN

Shamans are people who don't have their own magic power, but instead borrow power from the world around them. Tarras is an example of a Shaman--he uses the element Earth. He is part of a family that passes this earth knowledge down from generation to generation. Tarras was recently appointed to learn the secrets of his family.

WITCH

These are witches who decided to side with humans. The WH witches gathered all the magic and information that the WHs use to fight, and the WH would never be able to defeat enemy witches without their help.

IT'S THE MANA GUN!

MUTANT

Within the WH, mutants hold the strongest grudge against witches. They are people whose bodies have been modified by witches—mostly as the forced test subjects of witches who tried to turn them into supporters.

Many mutants who manage to escape from their witch captors join the ranks of the WHs. Words is a mutant who killed the witch who modified his body (you can probably tell which of his body parts has been changed...) Strangely enough, Tasha is also technically a mutant because he received a modified weapon from a witch.

Q & A

Q1: How did you come up with the clothing designs? (from mirinae)

A1: Many of my design ideas come from a Japanese manga I enjoy. I get some ideas from magazines that feature black and white fashion. I also keep up-to-date with the different styles of military uniforms around the world. A surprising number of my ideas come from military uniforms. ^^

**Q2: Are there any girl human WHs?
(from ChungPoomMyungWhul)**

A2: There are some, but only in Division 2's C-class and D-class, none in the Battle classes S, A, and B. All girls possess some innate magic, but normal human girls can't gather enough to become witches. They can train themselves to increase their mana, but any natural type female WH who is skilled enough to join the B-class has gathered enough mana to awaken as a witch. The same applies to female shamans and mutants.

Q3: In the first volume, Tasha contacts the Center to initiate HELP. How does one normally contact the Center? By cell phone? This world doesn't seem like it would have cell phones, though... (from Lucky)

A3: Yes, he has a cell phone. Diana has created a network of cell phones that are connected through magic. In my manhwa, technology doesn't match up with the real world. That's because the people use witches' magic in place of science. ^^; The cell phones in this world don't have buttons; since they're magic, they respond to voices, or even will. They are made specifically for a single user and no one else can use them. If a non-WH finds a WH's cell phone, they won't even know what it is.

Q4: Please tell us the name of the mind-controlling witch. (from Lucky-D.S)

A4: That poor witch, there was never a chance to include her name. It was..."Vanice Grebake"!
It's Northern European... I chose such an extravagant name, and it never even saw the light of day...